Andrew Bridges

CLEAN AIR

Rb
Flash
Point

ROARING BROOK PRESS

NEW YORK

Clean
Air

Contents

[1] OUR AIR

Air. It's easy to forget it's there. You can't see it. You can't touch it. You can't taste it or smell it. But every few seconds, you breathe it in to stay alive—your body needs the oxygen. And air does more. It moves water around the planet and rains it down to nourish all living things—plants, microbes, and animals. It helps keep Earth warm, and it protects us from the Sun's harmful ultraviolet rays.

But people have been pouring pollutants and greenhouse gases into the air. It's easy to think these pollutants just vanish—yes, into thin air! But add enough of them and we can all see, smell, and feel their effects. We'd better take better care of this precious resource—our air.

The Air Overhead

Our air is special. It has oxygen for us to breathe and an ozone layer to protect us. It traps some of the Sun's heat to keep us warm day and night. And it moves water around the globe for all living creatures—including us—to drink.

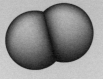

O_2
Oxygen

Every Breath You Take . . .

Whoosh. Air is sucked into your lungs. The oxygen molecules in that gulp of air are the reason you (and lots of other living things) breathe. Once oxygen is in your lungs, it floats into your bloodstream, hitches a ride on a red blood cell, and is carried to your cells.

. . . Every Move You Make

Muscle cells help you kick soccer balls, nerve cells help you solve algebra problems, and skin cells help you fend off bacteria. All that work takes energy. What's the best way to produce energy? With oxygen! Think campfires and rockets—gotta have oxygen for them to burn. Your clever little cells use oxygen to break apart sugar molecules. This releases energy to keep you going.

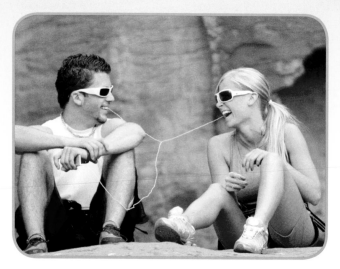

Earth's Sunscreen

Ozone! It's a good gas. If it weren't in our air, we couldn't go outside in the sunshine. The ozone in the atmosphere absorbs much of the ultraviolet light that the Sun continuously sends our way. If that ultraviolet light got down to us on Earth, it would damage our cells and the cells of other living things. Then we'd all be in trouble. And no, sunglasses wouldn't help.

H₂O
Water

H₂O in the Air

Water makes up two-thirds of every living creature, whether its body is just a single cell like an amoeba's or trillions of cells like yours. Being thirsty is a sign of life. Every person, microbe, tree, bird, fish, insect, and lizard must slurp water to replenish what's lost breathing, moving, and digesting. Fortunately, water loops around Earth through the water cycle—from the air to the land to the oceans, and back again. So water in the air comes down as rain or snow and fills ponds and streams for all of us who need it. Thirsty?

N₂ – Good for Anything?

Nitrogen gas (N_2) is packed in every breath we take. But it's in a form that we (and most other living things) can't use. Thousands of times each day, we breathe in N_2 and then breathe it right back out. Fortunately, a few types of bacteria floating in streams and hanging out in soil can suck in N_2 from the air and turn it into ammonia. When the ammonia leaks into the soil or water, plants soak it up. They use it to make amino acids, proteins, and DNA. Whew! Now all you (and other animals) have to do is chew on a salad or munch on an apple—and your body will have its share of nitrogen, too.

Greenhouse Gases, Good Guys?

They *can* be good—at least in moderation. There are small amounts of greenhouse gases like water vapor, carbon dioxide, and methane in the air—from natural as well as human sources. They trap some of the heat that Earth's land and oceans absorb from the Sun and try to send it back into space. Although those few molecules make up only a tiny bit of our air, without them Earth would be about 33°C (59°F) colder than it is! Penguins would be snow skiing in Hawaii (left).

Being There

Better Hold Your Breath

Earth wasn't always such a friendly place. If you ever get transported back 3 billion years in time, be sure to bring an oxygen mask! You wouldn't find any oxygen in Earth's early atmosphere. Back then, our planet's air was mostly carbon dioxide, nitrogen, and water vapor.

This drawing shows Earth as it might have looked about 4 billion years ago.

Water World

Three billion years ago, life was still wet behind the ears—it was all underwater. Way back then, the only living things on Earth were microscopic, single-celled creatures that lived in the sea. And there was no oxygen in the air. Then, eventually, some of those primitive microbes aquired the ability to use the Sun's energy to turn carbon dioxide and water into sugar for food. As part of this process, called photosynthesis, they released oxygen. Oxygen molecules began bubbling out of the water and drifting into the air.

Little Green Geniuses

What a great idea! Photosynthesis was nature's ingenious way of harnessing energy from sunlight to make food. Over the next two billion years, Earth's air filled with oxygen. Today, all the phytoplankton in the ocean and all their plant relatives on land carry out photosynthesis. So the oxygen in our air is replenished day in and day out. No oxygen mask required!

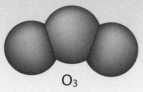

O_3
Ozone

Oh, Oh, Oh—That's Ozone!

Almost all oxygen in our air is in the form of O_2 molecules—two atoms of oxygen, happily bound together. But high up in the atmosphere, high-energy sunlight—sunlight that, fortunately, doesn't make it to the ground—breaks apart some oxygen molecules. That leaves a few oxygen atoms wandering around alone. Some of them hook back up with each other to form oxygen, but some link up with existing oxygen molecules to form O_3—ozone. Before the ozone layer formed, plants and animals had to live in the water to be protected from the Sun's ultraviolet rays. If there were no ozone layer, we'd all have gills and fins.

FROM THE GROUND UP

When you look up into the sky, it looks like the air goes on forever. But look at it from space, and you can see how little of it there is. If Earth were a tennis ball, the air would be thinner than the fuzz covering the ball. Earth as a tennis ball? Wouldn't bounce very well.

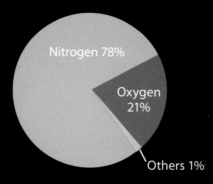

Nitrogen 78%

Oxygen 21%

Others 1%

So, What *Is* Air?

Air! What's air? Mostly nitrogen and oxygen. About 78 percent (78 out of 100) of the molecules in our air are nitrogen molecules. About 21 percent (21 out of 100) are oxygen molecules. Together, they make up about 99 percent of our air.

Forget Me Not

Yes, 99 percent of all the molecules in our air are either nitrogen or oxygen—but don't forget the gases that make up that other one percent. They include carbon dioxide, methane, and ozone—and we need them!

Sucking Air

No, you can't slurp it in through a straw, but our air also has water in it. Water vapor, that is. When scientists talk about air, they usually describe it as the combination of dry air and water vapor. That's because water vapor varies drastically from place to place, from day to day, and even from hour to hour. So it's a different percentage of the air depending on where you are and when you're there. You've heard of humidity? That's a measure of the water vapor in the air. Live in the desert? There's not very much humidity—it's dry! Live in Houston? In the summer, it can be like walking through a steam room.

Next time you're in an airplane, don't open the window for some fresh air! There's not much of it that high up. The air gets thinner and thinner as you go up. Airplanes are pressurized—they carry their air up with them, and the cabin is sealed to keep it from leaking out. And just in case, those funny little masks will drop down.

Tropo-*What?*

Most of our air—almost 90 percent of it—is in the layer of air that goes from the ground to just above the highest clouds. It's called the troposphere. All our weather—wind, rain, thunder, and lightning—is in the troposphere. It's where airplanes fly, dust swirls, eagles soar, and flags flutter. By the way, when we release stuff into the air, it goes into the troposphere.

> The troposphere extends about 8 kilometers (5 miles) into the sky above the poles and 16 kilometers (10 miles) high above the equator.

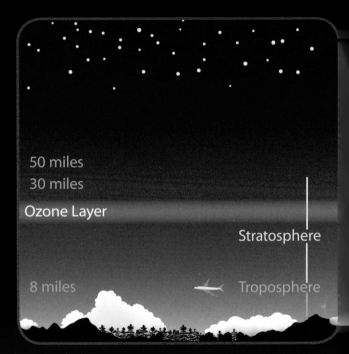

50 miles
30 miles
Ozone Layer

Stratosphere

8 miles

Troposphere

Blowin' in the Wind

Winds blow air around and mix the air in the troposphere. Ash from a volcano in the Philippines will blow over Alaska; pollution from China shows up in Los Angeles; dust storms in Africa blow iron to the Pacific Ocean. Next time you get a speck in your eye, check its passport—it might have just blown in from the mountains of China or the deserts of Africa.

The stratosphere begins where the troposphere ends. It stretches from about the tippy-top of Mount Everest to about 50 kilometers (30 miles) above sea level. It holds most of the rest of our air. But there's not much air up there, and almost no weather. The air in the stratosphere isn't very sociable—it doesn't mix with the lower air of the troposphere. Why even mention the stratosphere? That's where the protective ozone layer is.

Electrifying Scent

Ozone is made of nothing but good old oxygen atoms—but ozone is a rare molecule. The normal oxygen we breathe is made of two atoms of oxygen and is odorless. Ozone is formed out of three oxygen atoms and has a very distinct odor. If you've ever been caught in a thunderstorm, you may have smelled ozone. The gas can form when lightning strikes. Zap!

The O Zone

Ozone may be rare, but it's crucially important. It absorbs a form of energy from the Sun called ultraviolet radiation and prevents it from reaching the Earth's surface. Ultraviolet radiation can damage the cells of living things. It can reduce phytoplankton populations in the ocean, damage crops in fields, and even cause skin cancer in people. If you have ever slathered on sunscreen or put on a pair of shades, you can appreciate how the ozone layer helps shield us from the Sun. O, Thank you.

A Little Does a Lot

Even in the so-called ozone layer there's not much . . . ozone. For every 10 million molecules of air, over 2 million are the normal molecular oxygen we need—and just 3 are ozone molecules!

4 U 2 Do

Edible Air

What does our air and a fruit salad have in common? Mix up your own model of the air. Open your refrigerator and find three different-colored "molecules"—maybe grapes, berries, and chunks of apple. Anything about those sizes will work. Count out 100 pieces, dividing them into three piles—based on their percentage in the air. One pile for nitrogen, one for oxygen, and one for the trace gases. How many do you have in each pile? Now mix them all up. That's the atmosphere—a fruit salad of gases. Chow down.

Hint: Put your favorite molecule into the nitrogen pile.

Check out your answers on page 40.

CHANGE IN THE AIR

People didn't have much effect on the air until about 200 years ago. Then things started to change. People began to burn coal, oil, and natural gas—to heat homes and buildings, generate electricity, and power cars. Industrial plants spouted soot and chemicals (left). Fertilizers, pesticides, and refrigerants all released different chemicals into the air. At first, it didn't seem like a problem—there's a lot of air, and these chemicals just seemed to disappear into the sky. But eventually, all the living things on Earth started to feel the effects.

Fuel's Gold

You've heard of fossil fuels? Yes, they began as . . . fossils—fossils of plants and animals that lived in prehistoric oceans and swamps. Over millions of years, the decayed remains were buried deep underground and slowly cooked into coal (right), oil, and natural gas. Today, over *85 percent* of the world's energy comes from these fossil fuels. Coal is burned in power plants to produce electricity. Oil is refined into gasoline that goes to fuel our transportation. Natural gas is piped into homes for heating and cooking. But maybe we're just fossil fools. . . .

Fossil Fuelish

Burning fossil fuels produces energy to fuel cars, light offices, and heat homes. Why do we choose them instead of other forms of energy? Well, they're pretty easy to get, convenient to transport, and can be stored for later use. And, they're currently one of the cheapest forms of energy. Ah, but there's a problem. The chemical reactions in burning fossil fuels release energy. But they also produce gases and particles that can drift into the air—and they're doing damage.

If U Can C Your Air . . .

That's not good. Some coal power plants, diesel engines, industrial smokestacks, and even backyard barbecues, release soot and other microscopic particles into the air. That chicken may smell good, but the soot is gunking up lungs around the planet. As a result, more children everywhere are developing asthma and other breathing problems.

How Do They Know?

So Tiny, So Harmful

Good things come in small packages? Well, not always. Scientists have found that some of the most harmful damage to young lungs can be caused by very tiny particles in the air called aerosols. Some are produced by natural events, such as volcanoes and forest fires. But people add a lot of aerosols to the air—think dust from construction sites, exhaust from truck tailpipes, and smoke from neighborhood chimneys.

Right Under Your Nose

Worried about those big particles? They're not the problem. They may get blown into your eyes and make it hard to see, but they're too big to stay in the air for long. The medium-sized particles? They get trapped in that great filtering system—your nose. But the smallest particles, those about thirty times smaller than the thickness of a human hair, go straight in and get stuck deep in your lungs. Once they're lodged there, they make it more difficult to get a breath, and they are responsible for asthma attacks and irritation of the lungs.

4 u 2 Do

Breathing Not So Easy

You want to see aerosols at work? Go outside on a windy day. Using a jar with a lid, try to capture some of the dust floating around. You will be able to see some particles with your naked eyes. For the smaller ones, you will need a magnifying glass. Predict what you will see. Then look closely and draw what you observe. Those jagged little particles are the things that we all breathe every day.

Being There

When Pigeons Breathe

When you (or, for that matter, a poodle, pigeon, or porpoise) breathe, you don't want to inhale invisible chemicals that can irritate your airways, inflame your lungs, or even float into your bloodstream, causing chaos elsewhere in your body. Yet around the world, far too many people live in places with toxic ozone, sulfur dioxide, and nitrogen dioxide in the air from cars, factories, and power plants. Yuck! With every breath—about 10,000 each day—all those chemicals pour into your body.

A smoggy day in Pittsburgh, Pennsylvania.

Bad Air Day

You've probably had one. That's when the air in your town is so loaded with smog and other crud that even healthy children and adults are told to stay indoors. Sounds like science fiction—but most American cities have bad air days every year. Fresno, California? As many as 101 bad air days. Buffalo, New York? 36. And in booming Beijing, China, 165! Oh, my stinging eyes and burning throat.

Oil and Vinegar

In heavily industrialized areas of the U.S., China, and Great Britain, sulfur dioxide wafts out of smokestacks, and nitrogen oxide puffs out of tailpipes. These chemicals—a result of burning coal or oil—mix with water droplets in the air to form sulfuric acid and nitric acid. The droplets eventually fall back to Earth—as acid rain. The wind carries pollutants hundreds or even thousands of miles, where they fall on forests, lakes, and streams that were once pristine. So the bad stuff in the air can rain down and affect unsuspecting plants and animals, too. In some parts of the world, scientists have measured rain more acidic than vinegar. Oil and vinegar—sounds like a salad dressing. But keep reading . . . the U.S. and some other countries are putting a stop to acid rain by capping certain emissions.

It's easy to see which branch of pine tree needles is healthy and which is damaged by acid rain.

Not Just for the Birds

All rain is slightly acidic. But it's not good when rain gets *too* acidic. If you were a fern, a ladybug, or a mouse, would you want dilute acid falling into your drinking water? Of course not! Plants, insects, and small animals that live in or around water can be harmed and even killed by rain that is too acidic. Give that mouse a hazmat suit.

Being There

Last One off Venus Is a Rotten Egg

Venus may be our sister planet, but it is *not* a vacation spot. Never mind that the temperature is over 427°C (800°F). Volcanoes spew sulfur—famous for its rotten-egg odor—into the air as sulfur dioxide. The result? Layers of clouds made of sulfuric acid. Phew!

The air surrounding Venus is so thick you can't see the surface.

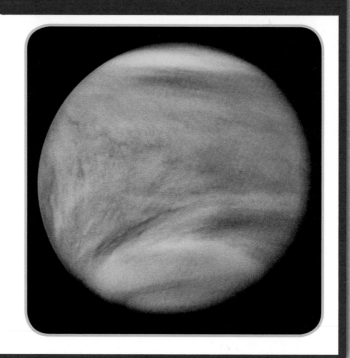

Acid Rocks

Most fish don't like swimming in acid. Who can blame them! In Sweden, thousands of lakes became so acidic that the fish died. In Germany, whole forests have been wiped out. The damage is not limited to fish and forests. Some buildings don't like acid rain either. The Parthenon in Greece (above) and the Taj Mahal in India have both been damaged by acid rain. The acid eats away at the rocks they're built from and leaves lots of little holes. That's the pits.

4 U 2 Do

Taking the Measure of Acid Rain

You can measure the acidity of the rain that falls on your school. First, you'll need some litmus paper—you can buy that at a drugstore. Next time it rains, collect some rainwater in a cup. Then dip a strip of litmus paper in the water. If the water is acidic, the strip will change color—it will turn red.

[4] THE HOLE AT THE POLE

In 1985, British scientists working in Antarctica noticed that each spring, the amount of ozone in the stratosphere over the South Pole dropped dramatically. This quickly became known as the ozone hole. No, it isn't really a hole in the atmosphere. But ozone levels dip by 60 percent when the hole opens up. That allows up to twice as much damaging ultraviolet radiation to reach Earth's surface below the hole. Not good for the penguins, plankton, and seabirds.

Experts Tell Us

Susan Solomon

Atmospheric Scientist National Oceanic and Atmospheric Administration

The ozone hole was a puzzle—but not for long. Scientists quickly began coming up with theories—and Susan Solomon's turned out to be the right one. The culprits were chlorofluorocarbons—CFCs for short—that people had created for refrigerants and a variety of other uses. "I was excited by the discovery. But I was also stunned to realize that it could have major implications for the world. It was a moment of awe, " Susan says.

Susan got turned on to science watching the deep-sea adventures of Jacques Cousteau. In school, she became an expert in the chemistry of the atmosphere. You might say her head's been in the clouds ever since! Susan can't rule out any more surprises like the CFC-ozone hole link, but thinks it's unlikely. "Today, we monitor the atmosphere much more closely that we did in the 1980s—so we have a better early warning system," she says.

Good Gases Gone Bad

Chlorofluorocarbons—CFCs—weren't always bad. They were developed as miracle chemicals for use in spray cans, refrigerators, and air conditioners. They're nontoxic, cheap to make, and last a really long time. When released into the atmosphere, they drift around in the troposphere for years and don't interact with anything. After many years, they eventually get carried into the stratosphere. It's up there that they start to cause problems.

Total Ozone (Dobson Units)

| 110 | 220 | 330 | 440 | 550 |

The satellite image (above) shows the amount of ozone over Antarctica in September 2007. Blues and purples are where there is less ozone; greens and yellows are where there's more.

Bad Breakup

Once CFCs make it to the stratosphere, the Sun's high-energy rays—rays that don't make it down lower—break up the CFC molecules and free chlorine atoms. Yep, that's the same stuff that's in your neighborhood swimming pool. It's a chlorine atom that starts a chain of chemical reactions that ultimately results in the loss of an ozone molecule. But here's the really bad news. At the end of that chain reaction, the chlorine atom is still around—ready to go off and destroy another ozone molecule. Just one chlorine atom can destroy more than 100,000 ozone molecules. Now *that's* a problem.

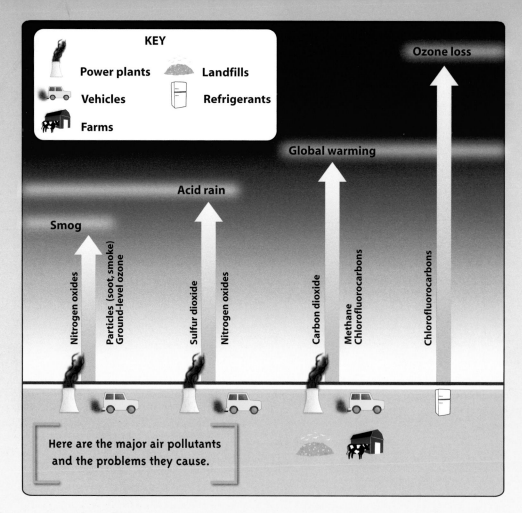

Here are the major air pollutants and the problems they cause.

Ban on the Run

Before 1987, anytime you used an aerosol can—like hairspray—or changed the coolant in your car, CFCs blew into the air. Not anymore. Once scientists realized how harmful CFCs could be, it didn't take long for the world to unite. In 1987, more than 100 countries signed an agreement called the Montreal Protocol to limit how much of those chemicals could be made and released. The ban is working—levels of chlorine in the air have begun to go down. Let's keep it in swimming pools, instead.

The Hole Truth

But the ozone hole still shows up over Antarctica every year. It hasn't even begun to shrink much yet. In 2007, the hole that opened was still the size of North America. That's because once CFCs get into the stratosphere, they stick around for a really long time. Some of the CFCs responsible for destroying ozone today escaped from your grandfather's can of spray paint 50 years ago. The ozone hole will be with us for a while. It will probably reappear every year until at least 2070.

Slips Along the Way

Some countries, including China and India, were given extra time to phase out CFCs and other related chemicals. But the demand for air conditioners and refrigerators in those countries skyrocketed faster than people expected, and so have their CFC emissions. Some scientists are worried that we're slipping in the war against CFCs. If so, the ozone hole will take even longer to patch.

In hot places like India, air conditioning units are selling like hotcakes.

Brown air over London means lots of ground-level ozone. And lots of Londoners with stinging eyes.

Ozone's Twin

Ozone's good, right? Yes, unless we have to breathe it! High in the stratosphere, ozone is "good." No lungs up there! But at ground level, it's not. Ozone is a major component of smog. Where does ground-level ozone come from? Round up the usual suspects—emissions from automobiles, power plants, and industrial smokestacks. They release compounds that react with each other and with sunlight to form ozone. Ground-level ozone is chemically the same stuff as the ozone in the stratosphere, but unfortunately when we come in contact with it, it irritates eyes, causes coughing and wheezing, and can even damage lungs.

CHANGING THE CLIMATE

The greenhouse gases in our air help make Earth a pleasant place to live. But now, you might say, we've got too much of a good thing. A little carbon dioxide in the air is good. But a lot is not. The more carbon dioxide or other greenhouse gases added to the air, the more heat is trapped—and the warmer the planet gets. That's what's happening now. And it's changing things all over our planet.

Planes, Trains, and Automobiles

. . . all burn gasoline. Streetlights, televisions, and refrigerators all use electricity—much of it generated by coal-burning power plants. Turn up the heat on a cold winter day? You're probably burning natural gas. Whenever fossil fuels like gasoline, coal, and natural gas are burned, carbon dioxide and other greenhouse gases are added to the air.

[
Bumper to bumper, cars and trucks pass under the Arc de Triomphe in Paris, France.
]

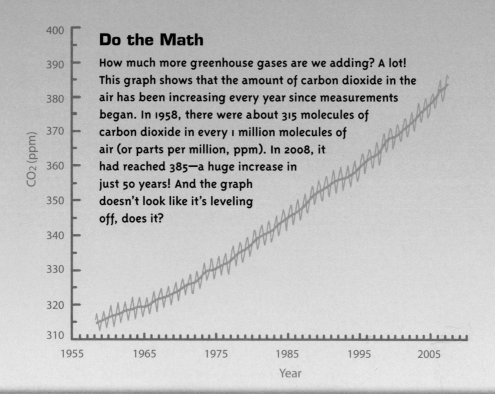

Do the Math

How much more greenhouse gases are we adding? A lot! This graph shows that the amount of carbon dioxide in the air has been increasing every year since measurements began. In 1958, there were about 315 molecules of carbon dioxide in every 1 million molecules of air (or parts per million, ppm). In 2008, it had reached 385—a huge increase in just 50 years! And the graph doesn't look like it's leveling off, does it?

4 U 2 Do

Up and Up

If we don't do anything differently, how much carbon dioxide will be in our air by 2050? Take a piece of graph paper. Trace the average line of the graph (the purple line). Now extend it to 2050. How much carbon dioxide will be in the air?

How Bad Is It?

It's not good. Today, the carbon dioxide level is higher than it's been in at least 650,000 years (yes, 650,000 years ago!). Now *that's* a long time.

All Together Now—Breathe

Want evidence that plants take in carbon dioxide during photosynthesis? Look at the squiggles in the graph. The amount of carbon dioxide goes down every spring and summer, then back up every fall and winter. In the spring, the plants in the northern hemisphere (where most of the land is) suck in carbon dioxide, grow, and flower. In the fall, leaves drop from the trees, and many plants go dormant. The squiggles show plants inhaling carbon dioxide, and then exhaling it six months later.

Up in Smoke

There's another way we add carbon dioxide to the air— burning or cutting down trees. Those trees, like all plants, take carbon dioxide out of the air for photosynthesis and store the carbon in their trunks, branches, and leaves. But when they're burned, or when they decay after being cut down, that carbon is released back into the air—as carbon dioxide. Deforestation? Bad idea! If you cut down a tree, plant another.

It's Not Just CO$_2$

Remember methane? It's a greenhouse gas, too. There is twice as much methane in the air today as there was 200 years ago. Methane bubbles out of swamps. It wafts up from rice paddies, swamps, landfills, and sewage treatment plants. And did you know that cows and sheep belch methane? There are eight times more people on the planet now than there were two centuries ago. So we grow way more rice, raise lots more animals, and produce tons more waste than we did back then. A lot more work for the garbage collector, and a lot more methane in the air.

Terraced rice fields in Guangxi Province, China.

Seemed Like a Good Idea at the Time

Fertilizers. They were created to help farmers increase the yield of their crops. But wouldn't you know it? Fertilizers also give off nitrous oxide. Yep, it's a greenhouse gas. Want another example? CFCs were a scientific breakthrough—perfect coolants for refrigerators and air-conditioning units. Now they're best known for causing damage to the ozone layer—but they're also powerful greenhouse gases. Who knew?

How Do They Know?

Earth on a Budget

If you watch how much money you earn and how much you spend, you're on a budget. Earth's on a budget, too—an energy budget, that is. A satellite launched in the 1980s called the *Earth Radiation Budget Satellite* measures how much energy arrives at Earth from the Sun and how much Earth sends back out into space. Knowing how much comes in and goes out helps scientists understand Earth's greenhouse effect. You can bank on it.

Oops!

Now we've done it. We've added enough greenhouse gases to the air that we're changing Earth's climate. Over the last 100 years, our planet has warmed up about 0.8°C (1.5°F). That doesn't seem like a lot. But it's the fastest our global average temperature has changed in 1,000 years—and it's still going up. Think about it. When your temperature goes up 1.5°, you're running a fever. Now Earth's running a fever. Wonder if it gets to stay home from school.

CHANGE THE CLIMATE, CHANGE OUR HOME

So it's getting warmer. What's the big deal? Well, scientists have already measured changes all around the planet. The oceans are warmer. Glaciers and ice caps are shrinking or even disappearing. Sea levels are rising. Ocean chemistry is changing. There's more rain in places that already get plenty, and less rain in places that need it.

Out of Whack

Climates around the world are changing. And as a result, seasons are changing, too. Winter is getting shorter, spring is starting sooner, fall is coming later. Everything on the planet is affected in one way or another. Pine trees, penguins, and people have all adapted to live under particular conditions in particular climates. Now, plants and animals are scrambling to find new homes because the places where they live are different than they were just a few years ago.

No Doubt—Drought!

Dry areas are becoming drier. Heat waves are coming more often and lasting longer. Droughts are becoming more severe. As the land becomes parched, the trees and plants dry out. Dry leaves and shrubs make perfect fuel for fires. Once a spark—from a bolt of lightning or a campfire ember—ignites a fire, it can rage through a dry forest or desert and send wildlife fleeing. Fires also affect people. They can destroy homes and other buildings. And send clouds of soot and smoke into the air—more problems for your lungs. Even Smokey Bear may need a mask.

Dust Busters

Dry land + windy days = dust in the air. Gusts of dust create dust storms that fill the air, cover everything, and make it difficult to see and breathe.

During the Dust Bowl of the 1930s, this huge dust storm blanketed Stratford, Texas.

Beware of Thawing Land

Huh? That's right. About a quarter of the northern hemisphere is covered by frozen ground, or permafrost—ground that's been "perma"-nently frozen since at least the last Ice Age. But as the air warms, the permafrost is starting to thaw. As it does, the icy ground turns to mush. More troublesome, bits of frozen grasses in the permafrost soil can finally decay. As microbes digest these plant pieces, the carbon in the plants is released as either methane or carbon dioxide. More greenhouse gases into the air. A lot more. If all the permafrost in Russia thawed, the additional carbon dioxide would double what's in the air today.

Over the past 20 years, the permafrost of Tanana Flats, Alaska (top) has melted, turning the tundra into wetlands (bottom).

Your Nose Knows

All that extra carbon dioxide in the air? Plants like it—more carbon dioxide for photosynthesis. But some like it more than others. Guess which ones like it most. Weeds! Take ragweed. Doesn't it trigger hay fever and asthma? That's the problem. Higher carbon dioxide levels supercharge this prickly weed to grow bigger and to make more pollen. Ragweed (left) grows just about anywhere—from roadsides to riverbanks to empty lots. When it lets loose its potent pollen in late summer, watch out! One little ragweed plant can unleash up to 1 billion grains of pollen in a single season. There aren't even that many noses in America. The number of people with these conditions has jumped sky-high over the past few decades. Definitely nothing to sneeze at.

Roughly 40 million Americans suffer sneezes, sniffles, and itchy eyes from hay fever. About 20 million people endure asthma.

Don't Drink the Air

Satellites in space have been measuring the water content of the air for the past 20 years. The eyes in the sky show that the amount has been steadily increasing. That's because warmer air can hold more water—water that evaporates from the oceans and the land. You felt that yourself last time you were outside on a hot, muggy day. Guess what? Water vapor is a greenhouse gas—so more of it in the air may lead to even more warming. Scientists have concluded that there's a human fingerprint on this increasing humidity—yes, our carbon dioxide emissions are responsible. Maybe we should have worn gloves.

And What Goes Up

. . . comes down. That includes water vapor. With more of it in the air, rainstorms are already becoming more intense. Computer models predict even more extreme and more unpredictable weather in the future. That means stronger rainstorms, hurricanes, and tornadoes. Dorothy and Toto may be taking another trip—soon.

This twister touched down in Oklahoma.

Experts Tell Us

V. "Ram" Ramanathan

Atmospheric Scientist
Scripps Institution of Oceanography

Brown clouds? That can't be good. These clouds are brown from soot and a chemical soup of other gunk that pours from tailpipes, smokestacks, and cooking fires across south Asia. Not good for lungs. And guess what—not good for much bigger reasons, too. "What we used to think of as just air pollution is now a major climate issue," V. "Ram" Ramanathan says. Ram's team sent a fleet of small robotic airplanes flying in stacked formation to study the dirty clouds. Here's what they discovered: Brown clouds warm the air, which means they amplify global warming.

Since 1950, the air in south Asia has warmed by almost 1.6°C (3°F), up to several kilometers (miles) above the ground. What's up that high? Himalayan glaciers that are melting away. Once they're gone for good, billions of people could face drought. The good news? The soot and other particles hang around in the atmosphere for just days or weeks. So . . . cut the pollution, and kiss brown clouds bye-bye. "The fix would be immediate," Ram says.

WANTED: CLEAN, FRESH AIR

It's time for some good news. Several technologies and actions by communities and governments have already improved the air in many parts of the world. Others are providing hope for the future. And not a moment too soon!

Does Your Engine Purr?

Catalytic converters—known as cats to their friends—are a real success story. They are attached to the exhaust systems of cars and convert harmful emissions from engines into common, nontoxic gases. Cats were introduced in the U.S. in 1975. Since then, they have significantly reduced smog all over the U.S., especially in cities like Los Angeles and Houston. They're required in cars driven in the U.S.

Catalytic? Converter?

What does *that* mean? Most modern cars use a three-stage system to clean up exhaust. The first two stages use metals as catalysts—they get the chemical reactions going, but aren't used up in the process. The first stage uses platinum and rhodium in reactions that convert nitrogen oxides into harmless nitrogen and oxygen molecules. Then the converter gets rid of unburned hydrocarbons and carbon monoxide by burning them over platinum and palladium. The third stage monitors the exhaust and changes the fuel mixture to make sure it doesn't have too much gasoline or too much oxygen. Exhausting!

Mowing Down Emissions

Could lawn mowers be next? Gallon for gallon, lawn mowers emit over 90 times more pollutants than car engines. There's a move afoot in California to require catalytic converters on the engines of lawn mowers. Cool cats.

Let's Clear the Air

Sometimes laws have to be passed to get people to clean up their act. The Clean Air Act was passed by the U.S. Congress in 1970 for just that purpose. Under the act, the Environmental Protection Agency (EPA) is responsible for cleaning up air pollution. Has it worked? Judge for yourself.

Pollutants	1970	2006
Carbon monoxide	197 million tons	89 million tons
Nitrogen oxides	27 million tons	19 million tons
Sulfur oxides	31 million tons	15 million tons
Particles		dropped by 80%
Lead		dropped by 98%

Yeah! Pollution can be curbed—thanks to all the folks who pushed to get these results.

What About CO_2?

Umm . . . but what about carbon dioxide and the other greenhouse gases? Fast forward to 2007. That's when the Supreme Court ruled that the Environmental Protection Agency under the Clean Air Act must regulate these gases, too. Smart ruling.

Look, There R Mountains!

From Mexico City to Cairo, New Delhi to Shanghai, and from Bangkok to Tehran, air pollution is a huge problem in many cities around the world. Pollution from burning fossil fuels—gasoline to make cars go, coal to produce electricity, oil for heat—can make the air millions breathe downright dangerous. In places like Tehran, the surrounding mountains wall in the pollution and vanish in the haze (top). But the peaks are starting to emerge again as the pretty view they once were (bottom). Thanks to aggressive efforts to cut tailpipe emissions, ration fuel, limit traffic downtown, and increase the use of public transportation, the air's cleaner in the Iranian capital than it has been in decades.

Keep On Truckin'

What about trucks? They haul our food, gasoline, and products from farms, refineries, and ports to supermarkets, gas stations, and factories around the country. But lots of trucks = lots of pollution. Trucks are a target of pollution-control efforts around the country. The new engines being manufactured emit 50 percent less smog-forming compounds. Particulates have been reduced by 90 percent. Beginning in 2010, a new generation of engines will reduce emissions even more.

Smartway to Go!

Trucking companies that use less fuel are being certified by the Environmental Protection Agency as SmartWay carriers. By 2012, this program should save billions of tons of diesel fuel and eliminate 30–60 million tons of carbon dioxide emissions.

Who'll Stop the Rain?

In 1985, the U.S. acted to reduce acid rain by controlling emissions from power plants. Since then, coal-burning power plants have cut their emissions of sulfur dioxide and nitrogen oxides by millions of tons. Almost all of the more than 3,300 power plants in America now have pollution devices in place. The big winners? Fish and trees. Aquatic and forest ecosystems in places like western Pennsylvania (left) are rebounding—all because of this successful environmental program.

All Aboard!

A heart transplant for a train? Great idea—especially in Kazakhstan. Remove the heart of the old train—its fuel-guzzling, pollution-emitting old engine—pop in a new model, and what have you got? A train that's more fuel efficient, emits fewer pollutants, and requires less maintenance. Renovating one of these trains is the equivalent of taking 34 cars off the road in the U.S. for a year. Even better, engineers say the new trains need fewer timeouts for repairs. That allows them to work more days a year. One hundred renovated locomotives can do the work of 130 of the old ones! There's just one problem . . . the size of the stretcher.

Raise the Roof

Here's an idea: green your roof. Huh? Paint it green? No, landscape it! Putting soil and plants on the tops of apartment buildings, school gyms, public libraries, and ritzy hotels is a way to reduce the amount of energy those buildings use and suck some extra carbon dioxide out of the air. Soil provides great insulation, so the buildings stay warmer in the winter and cooler in the summer. That means less fuel burned for heat and air conditioners. And those plants up there do what plants do—suck in carbon dioxide for photosynthesis. Cities from Portland, Oregon, to St. Paul, Minnesota, and from London, England, to Potsdam, Germany, are trying this as a way to reduce the amount of fuel they use and help cool the air. Time to water your roof?

This is the roof of the California Academy of Science building in San Francisco. No kidding.

The Coal World, Breathing Hard

Half the world's electricity comes from coal. Coal is plentiful and cheap. But, it's also really dirty. Around the globe, old technology coal-burning power plants spew carbon dioxide, soot, and sulfur dioxide into the air. Those old fashioned plants aren't used much anymore in the U.S., but they are in many parts of the world. And some countries are rushing to build more to keep up with the growing demand for energy. What can be done? Start building more modern power plants and retrofit old ones with newer technology that pollutes less. That would help the whole world breathe a little easier.

Residents of Linfen, China, wear face masks to protect themselves from air pollution.

What a Gas

There's an even newer technology around that turns that dirty black coal into gas, so the cleaner gas can be burned. This technique uses less coal to make the same amount of electricity. And you know what that means . . . less carbon dioxide going into the air.

Building a Better CO_2 Trap

Hey, how about capturing the carbon dioxide before it goes into the air? Good thought! And lots of people are working on just that. Here's the idea. As the gas burns, trap the carbon dioxide and then pump it deep underground or under the seafloor where it will stay buried for thousands of years. How long before this carbon sequestration technique is ready for prime time? Stay tuned.

This natural gas plant off the coast of Norway pumps the carbon dioxide it produces deep under the seafloor.

Energizing Our Future

No matter what you do, you're going to release carbon dioxide when you burn fossil fuels. So let's find energy sources to replace them—energy sources that are cleaner and that release either much less carbon dioxide or, even better, none at all! There are lots of candidates—and people around the world are already using them!

This car runs on gas and electricity. The hybrid gets such good mileage, it's allowed to use the carpool lane.

This farm in Germany runs on solar power—a squeaky-clean energy source.

Whoosh. Wind power is the fastest growing energy source in the world.

Conserve Energy

The easiest places to save energy are where we spend most of our indoor time—home, work, or school. Even simple steps, like turning out the lights when you leave a room, can cut electricity use. Adjusting the thermostat to make sure a room isn't overheated or overcooled conserves energy, too. Being creative allows you to save more. Using a clothesline instead of the dryer keeps a major electricity hog penned up. In the summer, closing the blinds to block the Sun's warming rays keeps the air conditioner from having to work overtime. And skipping the elevator for the stairs won't exactly reduce your electricity bill enough to make you wealthy, but it'll sure keep you healthy!

Experts Tell Us

Gina Solomon

Senior Scientist
Natural Resources Defense Council

Clean air. Good health. Gina Solomon is driven by these goals. A big part of her research has been investigating contaminants and toxins, and their affect on humans. Her groundbreaking study at the NRDC and the Coalition for Clean Air revealed that children who ride a diesel school bus may be exposed to up to *four times* more toxic diesel exhaust than someone traveling in a car directly in front of it. But, overall, there's some good news. "We are seeing major improvements in air quality in California and other states. We've come a long way on air quality over the years," Gina says.

Many regions of the country have worked hard to reduce ozone and particulate emissions. New studies are suggesting that the ozone limits need to be reduced still further. "The current science shows the standards do not adequately protect health," she added. More needs to be done. Gina's advice, "You'll feel better if you act. So if you're worried about this stuff, get engaged so you can take action."

Gina prepares to test mold and toxin levels in the air after Hurricane Katrina hit New Orleans.

One Fine Day

Our air overhead is precious. Its special mix of gases makes Earth a livable world. Yet, over the years, people have changed the air—and not for the better. It's affecting our health and the health of our planet.

But there are many examples all over the world of people and governments waking up to the problems and coming up with solutions. We need more of that to get back our clean, fresh air.

atmosphere (n.) A layer of gases surrounding a planet or moon, held in place by the force of gravity. (p. 6, 8, 9, 13, 20, 21)

climate (n.) Prevailing weather conditions for an ecosystem, including temperature, humidity, wind speed, cloud cover, and rainfall. (p. 24, 27, 28)

fossil fuel (n.) Nonrenewable energy resources such as coal, oil, and natural gas that are formed from the compression of plant and animal remains over hundreds of millions of years. (p. 14, 15, 24, 33, 37)

greenhouse effect (n.) The warming that occurs when certain gases (greenhouse gases) are present in a planet's atmosphere. Visible light from the Sun penetrates the atmosphere of a planet and heats the ground. The warmed ground then radiates infrared radiation back toward space. If greenhouse gases are present, they absorb some of that radiation, trapping it and making the planet warmer than it otherwise would be. (p. 27)

greenhouse gases (n.) Gases such as carbon dioxide, water vapor, and methane that absorb infrared radiation. When these gases are present in a planet's atmosphere, they absorb some of the heat trying to escape the planet instead of letting it pass through the atmosphere, resulting in a greenhouse effect. (p. 4, 8, 24, 26, 29, 30, 33)

photosynthesis (n.) Process by which plants use energy from sunlight to convert carbon dioxide and water into food (in the form of sugar). Oxygen is released in the process. (p. 9, 25, 26, 30, 35)

phytoplankton (n.) Aquatic, free-floating, microscopic, photosynthetic organisms. (p. 9, 12)

pollutant (n.) A substance that is added to the environment (air, water, soil) and can lead to harmful effects for living organisms. (p. 4, 17, 32, 35)

Answer

4 U 2 Do, page 13
nitrogen, 78; oxygen, 21; trace gases, 1